I0790755

Chapter One: Your Thoughts

On April 19, 2019 I took action to resign from my day job. After six years in this rat race I finally broke the cycle of employment. Not only did I break it in my life, but also for the next generation. My thoughts in those few years were how I could build my empire. I am thankful and grateful for what I have. I will turn my yearly income into my hourly income. Your thoughts are powerful, and you are what you think about. My focus and energy were on how to create multiple sources of passive income when I had this 9-5 job. I was also trying to figure out how I could bring more value to the marketplace. I did not let my day job kill my dream. For instance, while I was there, I used my time wisely and wrote two books.

Always think big and never be satisfied. You should say thank you Almighty God every time you accomplish a goal and settle another one. The universe will never say no to you, and it will always give you everything you want. On April 5, 2019 at 10:00 am, the site supervisor came for a post check. After greeting each other, I came close to her ear and told her that I wanted to give her my two weeks notice. She said, "You hurt my feelings". We walked outside together because I did not want everybody to know. Remember there are three things that you are supposed to keep secret: your income, your relationship, and your

next move. When we were outside, I went to my

car to get my letter of resignation. I went to the

parking garage and grabbed the letter and when I

came back, she was sitting inside her car. I gave her

the letter and she asked when was my last day. I

told her April 19th. She shook her head and said

that they were going to miss me and that I was their

best employee. My response was that I will miss

you as well, but it is time for me to jump and focus

on my company. Then she asked me if I could train

the employee who would be taking over my

position. I told her that I would be glad to do that.

She said that the new employee must speak a

different language like you. I told her do not worry

and that she will find someone. I then gave her my

business card and wished her the best.

Chapter Two: Believe Before You See It

A few months ago, I was visualizing those very

moments every time I was sitting at that desk on

my job. Every morning my son Sam would call me

before he went to school. He would greet me and

ask me how I was doing. He would ask me where I

was. I would say that I was at the Department of

Social Services (DSS). He would then say that I

must quit and chase my dream. I always tell him

that I am sending you to school to be an owner not

an employee. He will never work for anybody. I

really mean it when I say it. I will make sure the next generation will never work for anybody. My children and my grandchildren will create jobs and provide a quality service. They will also bring more value in the marketplace. I believe that their purpose is to be great.

My son Sam was using my own words against me. He pushed me closer to my goal and because of him I broke this cycle of employment. Now I am so happy to use my passion and have multiple sources of passive income. I used to daydream at this desk. I would see myself walking in the parking lot and having a fleet of buses with my company's logo on them. I am shaking my employees' hands also giving them the keys to the buses and everybody was clapping for me and congratulating me. In my visualization, my wife and son are beside me. This event happened inside our property. I used to see a huge building with our logo on the top RSN Enterprises and an eagle. Guess what? Now we own buses and my imagination became a reality. What your mind believes, your mind can achieve it. Einstein used to say, "Your imagination is more powerful than knowledge". When you change the way you look at things, the things you look at will change. When I changed my habit of employment, my life changed. You do not get paid by time. You get paid for the value you bring to the marketplace.

Chapter Three: Take Action

Faith without action is dead. Be willing to always act regardless of what people around you say. When you have an idea, act quickly to bring it to reality. If you do not do it, this idea will go to someone else who will act and bring it to life. Then one day you will go somewhere and see your ideas displayed in a store. Maybe you procrastinated or you listened to people with a negative mental attitude (NMA). Never share your major goals with anybody. Life is an energy. If you share your ideas with negative or average people, they will attract negativity to you if you allow it. Stay away from people who are negative because like attracts like.

In 2017 I started using my imagination to create inventions and write books. I refused to procrastinate. Believe me it was not easy. Every time you try to reach another level or raise your standard, the enemy will use obstacles to keep you stuck where you are. God will never let you down. This battle is not yours, it's for God Almighty. God is our creator and we are his creation. He will fight for you and you will win this battle. Do not just sit still because you know God has your back. You must act and do your part and God will do the rest. Just be sure to act!

Chapter Four: Victim of Their Belief

Your imagination combined with your belief are two powerful tools to success that can bring your idea to reality. People are victims of their belief. For instance, in the jungle every morning a lion and a gazelle wake up. They both start running but the gazelle must run faster than the lion. If the gazelle does not outrun the lion, it will be eaten. Even the elephant who is big and strong is victim of his belief. The elephant believes it is lunch for the lion, but the lion's mindset makes him be the king of the jungle. Just like these animals, some people are victims of their own beliefs.

They probably grew up around losers or people who have a negative mental attitude. What you think about expands. If your thoughts are negative, you will receive negativity all around. Some people think being an entrepreneur is too hard and they end up be an employee until they die. They will work for someone else's dream. Warren Buffet said, "If the money does not work for you while you sleep, you will work until you die. I know some people get irritated when I advise them to open their own company. They think they are born to trade their time for money, something you should never do.

Chapter Five: Winner's Mindset

A winner never quits, and a quitter never wins. When we decided to open our company in the US, we had to climb a lot of obstacles on our way to success. Starting with what type of buses we want for the company. The first dealer we went to was nice to us, but his price was a little bit too high. My wife and I decided to shop around. A few days later we saw a nice bus online. We decided to call the dealership to make an appointment and the dealer was willing to see us soon as possible. The following Saturday we drove over an hour to get there. When we got there, we stayed inside the car for at least fifteen minutes in the parking lot. No one approached us to ask if we needed help. We decided to walk inside the lot and give ourselves a tour. We later saw the bus that we were looking for. We noticed the bus was running when we got closer. A gentleman came over and asked us if we were the couple that wanted to see the bus. We told him yes and asked if we could look at the interior of the bus. My wife went in first and I could see her body language and vibration change. When I got inside, I noticed at least three or four chairs were broken and the driver seat was shaking. There were a few parts on the floor and the engine was running rough. Remember your impressions and feelings never lie. My wife told me that she did not like it and all my response was we can fix it, but she was not willing to change her mind.

We approached this gentleman and asked him if he had more buses for us to see. He told us that he had a fleet of buses one or two miles away at a different location. We drove there and we saw a lot of the same buses. I told my wife that this is a sign of us being on the right path. My visualization always showed me a fleet of buses with our company logo parked in our garage. My wife said let's look inside. The dealer told us that no one was at this location because it's the weekend, but the doors should be open. He did not have the keys to start the buses. My wife and I followed him, and he opened the driver's door. We climbed over the driver's chair in order get inside. Almost all those buses were damaged inside except one or two. Almost all those buses did not pass the state inspection. After we left, I told him I was willing to buy all the buses under the condition they are inspected. He was honest told me he did not know if they had been inspected by the state and we would need to spend the money to repair them. I thank my wife, who is also my business partner, for telling me no. She said that we needed clean and great buses for the comfort of our customers. One night I was home around 7:30 pm and I decided to go on google and search for buses. I found several of them but only a few caught my attention. One of them was a coach bus that had a very nice

bathroom, television monitors and full options but

it had over 200,000 miles. The next day I tried the

search again and I found a nice one with low

mileage and that looked brand new with only one

owner.

Chapter Six: Never Give up

We called the dealership and we set up an

appointment. The dealer promptly approached us

when we arrived and started working with us. We

bought the vehicle the same day without even

seeing the vehicle physically. We only saw a

picture of the vehicle online. One of the managers

told us that the vehicle would be there in one or two hours. It was around 7:50 pm or 8:00pm. One of the salespeople came with the site supervisor and said that it was too late for the driver to bring the car to this location because of the traffic. They told us that we could come back the following day or they could deliver the vehicle to our house. We were a little bit disappointed and we decided to come back on the next day. They called us the next day to come pick up the vehicle. When we got there, the salesman gave us the keys and put the temporary tag on the vehicle. The night before we called our insurance company to make sure the vehicle had enough coverage. We told the company that we wanted to pay monthly, but they charged us for the whole year. We asked twice for the monthly plan and they assured us that was the way the payment was set up. We could not leave the dealer until the correct insurance papers were emailed to the car dealership. We stayed there for four hours just to solve this issue. The insurance lady said we had two options. The first one was to cancel the policy and wait four to five weeks to receive the refund by check. The second option was to create a new policy and pay for it that same day. The one-year policy she made us sign was a couple of thousands of dollars! The enemy will always try to stop you every time you try to accomplish something great in your life.

My wife and I trained our minds for these types of situations and how to respond. We stayed calm and meditated and released the insurance lady with the highest love. We let go of any negative thoughts that we had. They were free from us and we were free from them. Remember you can not change the way people treat you, but you can change the way you respond. We stayed inside the new vehicle for six hours until we asked the insurance lady if we could talk with her supervisor. The atmosphere began to change when her supervisor started talking with us. We told her that we had just bought a commercial vehicle and we were charged several thousands of dollars for a commercial policy. She partially solved the issue and we had to pay for them to start a new policy and cancel the policy that we had created the previous day. It was so easy for them to take the money from our account but, difficult for them to put it back. Jim Rohn said, "If you do what is easy your life will be hard, but if you do what is hard your life will be easy". We finally left the dealer around 8:00pm with our new company vehicle.

The next step was to apply for the DOT number. We applied for the intrastate number online and received it the same day. We needed to apply for the WMATC number next, but we needed to have all the documents before submitting the application. You must have a for hire registration and not the temporary registration before you can make an appointment for the inspection of the vehicle. You must pay and then wait four to seven weeks before they send you a letter letting you know that you have been granted a WMATC number. It takes two weeks for them to email you a response letting you know that they received your application. Imagine if you have had an average mindset. You would probably give up because they try to make things complicated for people to become owners. All the documents that you submit online must be in PDF format. They will reject the documents if they are not formatted correctly. The dealer called us almost every day for two months requesting for us to send him different types of documents. This was just the enemy trying his best to stop us. God has the final say. What your mind believes, your mind can achieve.

Chapter Seven: Iceberg

Success is like the tip of the iceberg that everybody can see. People cannot see the part that is deep in the water. They do not know how you got where you are. No one sees the failures, obstacles, rejections, tears, pain, brokenness or injuries. You should stay focused on where you want to go and not on what you fear. Zig Ziglar said, "Fear is just false evidence which appears to be real". My journey to become an entrepreneur was not easy. I knew one thing for sure, nothing is impossible for a child of God. God gives us the strength to accomplish anything we want. He will never give you a task if you cannot solve it. He is the alpha and the omega, the beginning and the end. He already has a solution for all your problems. Everything is in your vortex and cortex.

Chapter Eight: Time Management

Your time is a currency. The way you use your time determines your day and life. The beggar and the rich both have twenty-four hours in a day. The rich use their time to solve issues and provide a service for their customers and bring more value to the marketplace. The beggar uses his time to ask for help. They need to realize their God given talent and use their unique gifts to bring more value to the marketplace. Constantly giving money to a beggar will not help him. You will make him lazier especially if he is not handicapped or have a disability. If you really want to help him, you should teach him how to fish. As the saying goes, "If you give a man a fish he'll eat for a day, but if you teach him how to fish, he'll eat for a lifetime". Jim Rohn and Zig Ziglar both used to say, "When you give people what they want, you will have everything you want". Life will never give you what you want but what you deserve.

Andrew Carnegie once said, "There are three ways to use your time: sleeping, working and recreation". This man was the mentor of Napoleon Hill who write the book <u>Think and Grow Rich</u>. He was also one of the richest men in United States. You should always learn from the best. Andrew Carnegie was a philanthropic person. He gave his fortune to charities and built libraries around the world before he died.

Chapter Nine: Brainwaves

We are spiritual beings living in a human body. We have five brainwaves which control our brain. The first one is delta which means deep sleep. The second one is theta which means deeply relaxed. Alpha brainwave is for relaxation also. Beta brainwave is for focus or alertness. The fifth brainwave is gamma which is for high performance. When you are between the ages of one to six, your brainwaves are between delta, theta and alpha. At this time a child can learn three different languages easily and they can also learn one thousand new words. The average adult learns about five new words a year. Everything is determined between those ages such as their subconscious mind recording everything and believing it. For example, you should tell your child that he is great and can accomplish anything. He will believe whatever you say, and his subconscious mind will go to work take to make this thought become a reality. If you say some negative words to your child, he will also believe it. For example, your child may accidently spill something, and you yell at him. Next time he will be scared to do the same thing because his subconscious remembers everything. You should never yell at your child but have compassion and deep understanding of his action. Another example would be if you see your child working on a school project. You may start yelling at him because he is not focused. You should not scare him into doing things differently. You should support him by telling him that you are so proud of him and of his progress. Show him that he has greatness in him. He will become confident, focused and you will switch his vibration. Never criticize someone who is making progress because even the small progress is something. Next time he will be more creative and will use his vortex and cortex to solve tasks. He will be on a beta brainwave. When a child reaches the age of 6 to 7, he is not creative anymore because he is a victim of the belief of his parents or people around him. These people can tell him that he cannot have something, or he cannot do something. Your words are powerful so use them wisely and everything you think about will expand.

Your kids will value what you value and be careful of what kind of seeds you put in them. Every seed has a plant and every plant has a seed to maintain the future. You are raising someone else's father or mother. When your child was five years old, he used to tell you that he wanted to be an entrepreneur or an inventor. He used to have a lot of inventions, creativity and he his brainwave was at beta and gamma. Now he is twelve and his brainwave is at delta. This means his creativity and passion are asleep due to his negative thoughts and the negative people around him. I have great news for you. Your child still can reach his beta and gamma brainwaves if he changes his thoughts.

Chapter Ten: Reprogram Your Mind

You can reprogram your mind by closing your eyes and using your visualization. This will activate your reticular system. Next you need to imagine yourself having what you desire or accomplishing your goals. Visualize the feeling that you have when you accomplish your goals. You can do that every morning for just thirty seconds. This is called faking it until you make it. In the beginning you will have some resistance. Keep going and repeat the meditation for twenty-one days until your subconscious records it. Repetition is the mother law of learning.

Your visualization can help you build things. Thomas Edison used to sit in a chair with his eyes closed while holding a metal ball. While he was drifting into a delta brainwave sleep, he would drop the ball into a metal bucket. The noise of the ball falling into the bucket would wake him up and put him in the beta brainwave. Beta brainwave means being alert or focused. Every time that he did this, he would come up with new ideas. That means you can also reprogram your mind while you are at delta sleep brainwave. While you sleep, your conscious mind goes to sleep. Your subconscious mind can take over and work for you while you sleep to help you find new ideas.

Chapter Eleven: The Power of Your Subconscious Mind While You Sleep

Your subconscious mind works 24/7. Program your subconscious mind to work for you while you sleep. You can turn on an affirmation video or an audiobook which talks about what you want manifested in your life. The best way is to sleep with your earphones on as you listen to your auto suggestions or affirmations that are pre-recorded. Before going to delta wave say to yourself, "When I wake up in the morning, I will have everything I want". You can also say, "I command my subconscious mind to bring me……. (state what you want). Do not say need because that will sound like you are desperate. Believe your request will be answered when you wake up in the morning. Be thankful and grateful to God who gave you this privilege. Close your eyes and visualize yourself having what your heart desires. Imagine your employees or family members happy for your success. Visualize your bank account being filled up billions and billions of dollars. Open your eyes and let the universe work on your request. Faith without action is dead. You must act like the person you want to become. Surround yourself with people who do what you want to do. You can go to those places where they have what you want and use your visualization. See yourself having those things.

Chapter Twelve: Protect Your Brain

When you go to bed, please put your phone away. Please do not put you phone under your pillow. Ninety percent of children sleep with their cellphones under the pillow. This is not good for their brain.   Here are some of the worst foods for your brain health. Refined breads and pastas have been stripped of their nutrients so there's no fiber to slow down their digestion. Instead, these processed carbohydrates rush through your system and spike your blood sugar. Red meat, vegetable oils, cheese, refined sugar are some other foods that are not good for brain health. Not all carbs are bad! In fact, whole carbs are great for you. Whole grain breads, rice and pastas still have their fiber intact. That means they are digested more slowly. Your blood sugar is better regulated, and you therefore have a steady stream of energy so you can buckle down and focus. The most important dietary contribution to Alzheimer's disease appears to be meat consumption, eggs and high fat dairy.

Saturated fat clogs the cardiovascular system and the blood vessels in our brain becomes clogged as well. Instead you can skip the beef and make beans the center of your plate as a great source of protein! Beans are packed with brain boosting B vitamins and magnesium. Vegetable oils are high in Omega-6s, an inflammatory fatty acid. Consuming vegetable oils, particularly canola oil, increases the risk for Alzheimer's disease. Chronic brain inflammation is also linked with depression and other cognitive issues. When our brains are inflamed, energy production goes down. The firing of neurons is slowed down and we're often left mentally exhausted. You may find eating walnuts can help with mental exhaustion. Walnuts are full of the protective fatty acids Omega-3s. Omega-3 deficiencies can disrupt our ability to learn and retain memories. In fact, studies have found that dementia patients have low Omega-3 levels.

Pizza and cheese are the biggest sources of saturated fat in the American diet. As I mentioned with meat, saturated fat clogs our brain vessels just like it clogs our heart vessels. Higher saturated fat is also linked to inflammation of the brain. This contributes to higher risk of strokes and impaired memory. If you want to avoid heart disease and brain inflammation, eat avocados as a creamy and plant-based alternative to cheese. Avocados haves lots of potassium, which can improve blood pressure and reduce the risk of stroke. They're also a great source of folate. Folate deficiency is also associated with cognitive decline and Alzheimer's disease.

Americans eat way too much added sugar. Studies show that an average person eats nearly 66 pounds of refined sugar per year. Why is this an issue? Too much sugar causes inflammation in the brain. Just like those refined carbs, sugar can spike your blood sugar which leaves your body and your brain deprived of brain derived neurotropic factor (BDNF) levels. BDNF is crucial for learning and making new memories. Sugar is very addicting. Brain scans reveal that added sugar changes our brain chemistry in a way that looks very similar to our brains if we ingested cocaine or alcohol. An alternative to sugar could be whole foods, particularly blueberries, to help curb your sweet tooth. Eating berries may stave off short term memory loss due to their powerful antioxidants called anthocyanins. Power your day with a blueberry smoothie!

Chapter Thirteen: Your Thoughts Travel Faster Than Your Voice.

You must talk about what you want and not about what you do not want. Your words are powerful and everything you think about extends. Always be positive. Some people say stuff like, "I am not going to find parking, or the traffic is horrible". They are surprised when all these things they said happen. You must substitute those negative thoughts with the positive ones. For example, you must say, "I will find a parking space when I get there. The parking space is waiting for me". Visualize yourself parking your car in the spot you want.

God will always give you what you want. He is omniscient and omnipresent. He knows exactly what you want even before you say it. Always say what you want and be positive. This will separate you from average people who pass their time complaining and blaming others for their problems. God is the manufacturer and we are his products. Be very disciplined about what you think because that can impact your life positively or negatively.

Ask, believe and receive, those three words are

powerful. You just need to ask God or the Tao or

Allah what you want, believe and you can receive.

Chapter Fourteen: Build Your Character

On April 19, 2019 I decided to resign from my

day job to focus on my business because your

energy always goes where you focus. I faced a lot

of obstacles some of which you can't even imagine.

The field that we choose on this journey of

entrepreneurship had a lot of restrictions. For

example, we didn't know the transportation vehicle

required a 1.5-million-dollar insurance coverage in

DC if your vehicle is a 15-passenger vehicle. If the

vehicle is more than 15 passengers, you must have

a 5-million-dollar insurance coverage. When we

found out, we called the insurance company. They

raised the the monthly payment by 4 times. Then

the WMATC office wanted the insurance company

to send them the documents that proved that we

had the correct coverage. We paid the insurance

and they send those documents over to the

WMATC office. After the insurance has been

approved, you must go for the inspection. Then

someone from their office will send you an email

letting you know when to come in for the

inspection. This process took months and

remember you cannot operate your vehicle. You

still must pay the insurance and car note every month. You must be there on time and at the right location for your inspection. They do not give you an address. They only give you two street names that intersect. You are responsible for finding the exact location. I was scheduled for June 3 at 11 am. I was there at 10:40 am and I called the gentleman who was in charge when I arrived. When I called him again at 11:10 am, he did not answer the phone. He transferred me to the receptionist. She said, "Mr. C was out there at 11:00 am and he did not see you. You must reschedule your appointment for next Monday". Remember this is a commercial vehicle and you must provide a service in order to get paid. I decided to go inside the office to ask them if they could inspect the vehicle today because I had been here since 10:40 am. Mr. C said that I had to come back Monday because I wasted his time. I tried to explain to him where I was, and I asked why he did not answer his phone. He told me that he was not supposed to look for me. He said that I must be at the location that he told me. I thanked him and left his office. I took a picture of the vehicle and sent it to him to make sure that I don't waste his time again. He replied by email by saying that he cannot inspect the vehicle because I do not have the permanent decals and I must put the company name on the vehicle. It was on a Friday after 12 pm. I tried to reach multiple companies to put the permanent decal on but unfortunately no one was willing to do the job during the weekend. Most of them were willing to charge me a lot of money because I wanted the job done right away. I never take no for an answer and tried until I found one that was located an hour and a half away from our house. I went over there quickly. I sent a picture to Mr. C after the letters were installed on the vehicle. Mr. C said that the decals were acceptable. I went for the inspection on Monday and passed. I said all of this to say, never give up! When you are close to your goal, the obstacles will come from everywhere. This is a sign that you are on the right path. Everything that comes easy goes away just as easy. Zig Ziglar once said, "If you do what is easy your life will be hard and if you do what is hard your life will be easy.

Fear is the problem and love is the solution. We

must love the process that builds our character.

Thanks!

Thank you to those who have read my first two

books and asked for more. You gave me the

courage and belief that I could really do this.

Thank you to those who purchased my books and

made our sells grow.

Thank you to those who recommended my books to their friends and family members and continued to spread the word.

Thank you to everyone who sent me honest and kind words. This means more than you can imagine.

Thank you to everyone who has taken time out of their day to read it.

Thank you to my family, my wife, my sons, my sisters, my brothers, my nephews, my nieces, my cousins, my brother in law, my business partners and every single one of you who have supported me from day one. You have inspired me to continue to move forward and pursue my dreams.

You've brightened my dark days. You helped me believe that nothing is impossible, and I can do all things through God who strengthens me.

For all of this and for all of you amazing people, I will be forever grateful.

www.ingramcontent.com/pod-product-compliance
Lightning Source LLC
Chambersburg PA
CBHW051129250726

48655CB00007B/2962